BEST OF DAILY QUOTES
I AM THE CHANGE I SEEK
KATHLEEN SUNEJA

CM WELLS PUBLISHING
JACOBS WELL, QUEENSLAND
AUSTRALIA 4208
info@cmwellspublishing.com

I AM THE CHANGE I SEEK
THE BEST OF DAILY QUOTES with notes
Copyright 2018
KATHLEEN SUNEJA

First International Edition
ISBN: 978-0-6480052-9-2

All rights are reserved. No part of this publication may be reproduced, stored in a retrievalsystem or transmitted, in any form or by any mean, mechanical, photocopying, recording or otherwise, without prior written permission of the original publisher

Author's Note

Life comes with no rule book; each person figures out solutions to its challenges to survive, thrive and to find a purpose for existence in this life. In simple words, I share my thoughts on some fundamental ideas on the mysteries of life. In the following pages, I lay out timeless notions on appreciating and becoming self-aware of opportunities afforded on the profound, yet essential virtues of living. These quotes began as an attempt to reach out to all to explain and to help to appreciate life's journey. Doubtless each person endures its trials and tribulations, but one is richly rewarded from sharing this knowledge and wisdom with fellow persons so they too may benefit. Shared knowledge helps to overcome and resolve its challenges and keeps civilization from tripping on its own failures. There is no greater gift we can give each other than to share our wisdom because life belongs to those who have resolved its mysteries and conquered its turmoil. It is my humble duty to fulfill this responsibility to promote and provide successful guidance and the opportunity to succeed.
To lift all with such often self-evident, yet essential wisdom is often mundane, yet for those to who are familiar with this wisdom, let my words and quotes be a reminder and for all others, let them be new wisdom with which to renew life's work.

Life richly rewards us with the timeless bonds of friendship and the pleasures of shared love. The world of social responsibilities is often overwhelming; therefore, it is imperative to bring attention to the awesome genius and beauty of the natural world and to relate to it as well as to appreciate the demonstrable lessons it teaches by example. Nature guides us as we observe its genius, beauty and majesty so we can win our private battles and teach ourselves to right our wrongs; to take each opportunity to forgive and to build new bonds of love in relationships we hold dear so all may prosper and build for future generations.

Friendships and the love gained from relationships is perhaps one of our greatest gifts, without which we cannot survive. Bonding with nature is to bring the wonderment to each moment. Each person creates their own ideas and formulates their answers to questions of how, what, when and where about life. I attempt to provide answers to these questions in the following quotes.

Upon the recommendation of friends, I created an application on play store and istore called I Am the Change I Seek. My goal was to help others build a fulfilling and wonderful life with other fellow humans. Over time, I created many quotations which are currently available on the App. This led me to compile some of them into a book format which is called, The Best of Daily Quotes.

These concise quotes are meant to explain life's mysteries and give meaning and direction to readers with the purpose of living life more fully and to understand lessons from Nature as well as to give guidance on living a fulfilling life. They are meant to uplift and inspire readers in their daily lives. I fervently hope they fulfill this promise.

Kathleen Suneja

THE BEST OF DAILY QUOTES
NATURE

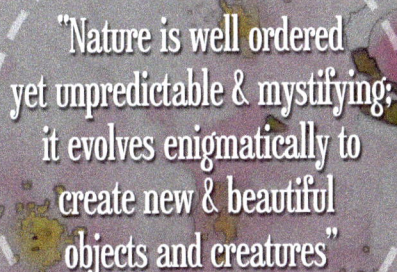

"Nature is well ordered yet unpredictable & mystifying; it evolves enigmatically to create new & beautiful objects and creatures"

Kathleen's Note:
Embrace yourself as one of nature's miracles

"Nature nourishes with its harvests so all can flourish and share"

Kathleen's Note:
Live and flow of all
Nature's boundless wealth

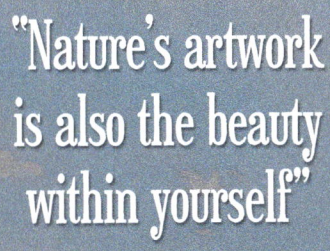

"Nature's artwork is also the beauty within yourself"

Kathleen's Note:
Explore your limitless potential to realize your beauty

"Become acutely concious of nature's unconditional giving"

Kathleen's Note:
As nature's gives us, so should we give of ourselves

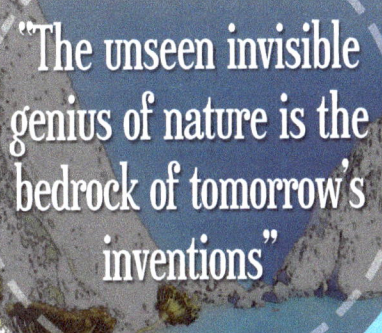

"The unseen invisible genius of nature is the bedrock of tomorrow's inventions"

Kathleen's Note:
Create for perfecting only that which is imperfectly made

"Observe nature's wisdom in the great outdoors"

Kathleen's Note:
Walk in nature often to observe, imbibe and admire it

"Accept nature's unspoken healing to renew with moments of bliss"

Kathleen's Note:
Become aware and be in tune with your natural healing abilities

> "Connect in spirit with nature's ways to find true wisdom"

Kathleen's Note:
In the quietly reveals its unlimited power and method in the process of creation

"Let the colorful and beauty of nature's seasons bring infinite joy"

Kathleen's Note:
The colors of spring, summer, autumn and winter soothe the soul to cheer up and brighten our lives

THE BEST OF DAILY QUOTES
FRIEND SHIPS

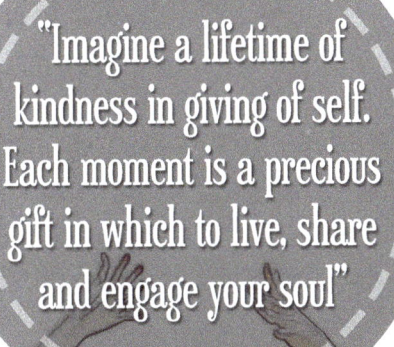

"Imagine a lifetime of kindness in giving of self. Each moment is a precious gift in which to live, share and engage your soul"

Kathleen's Note:
Make each moment count to bring joy to others

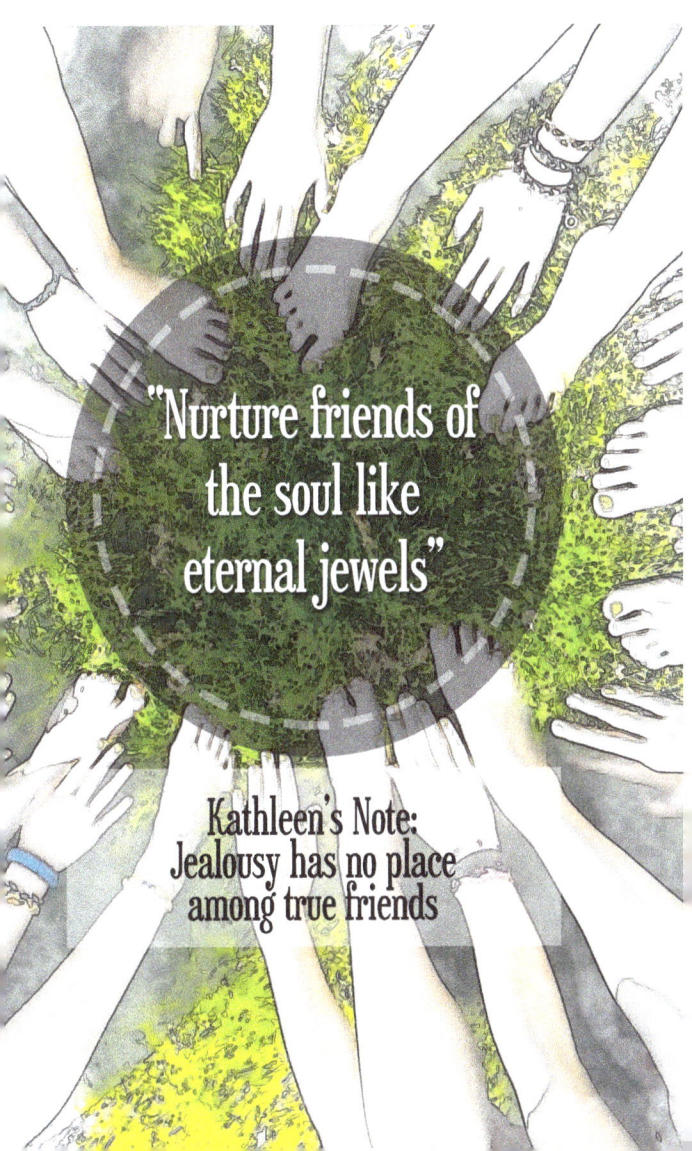

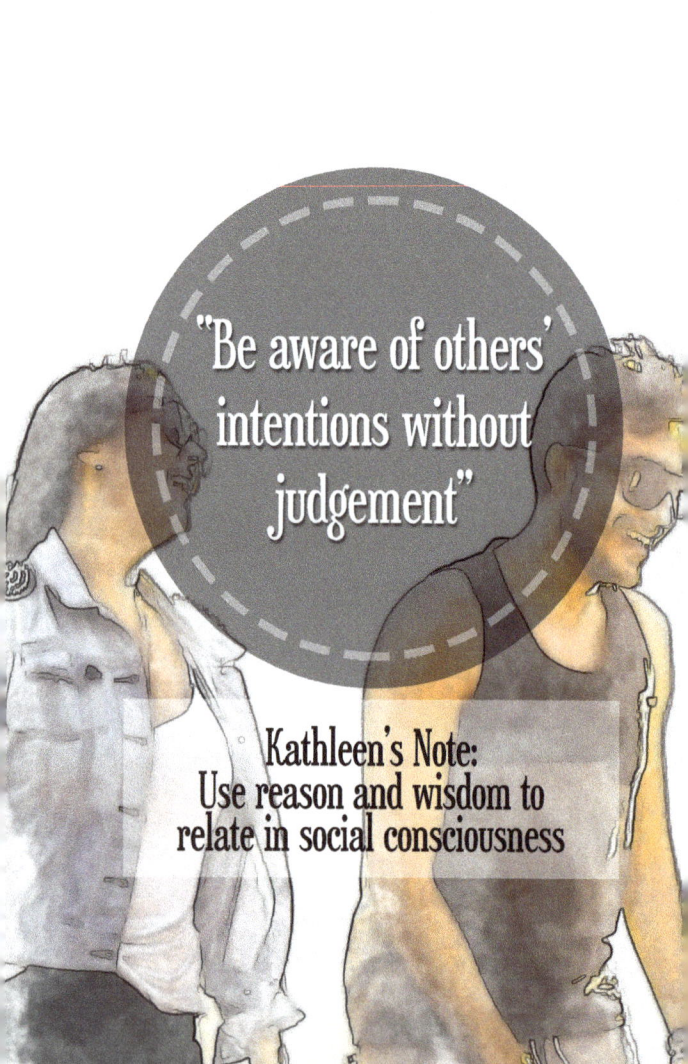

THE BEST OF DAILY QUOTES
TRUE SELF

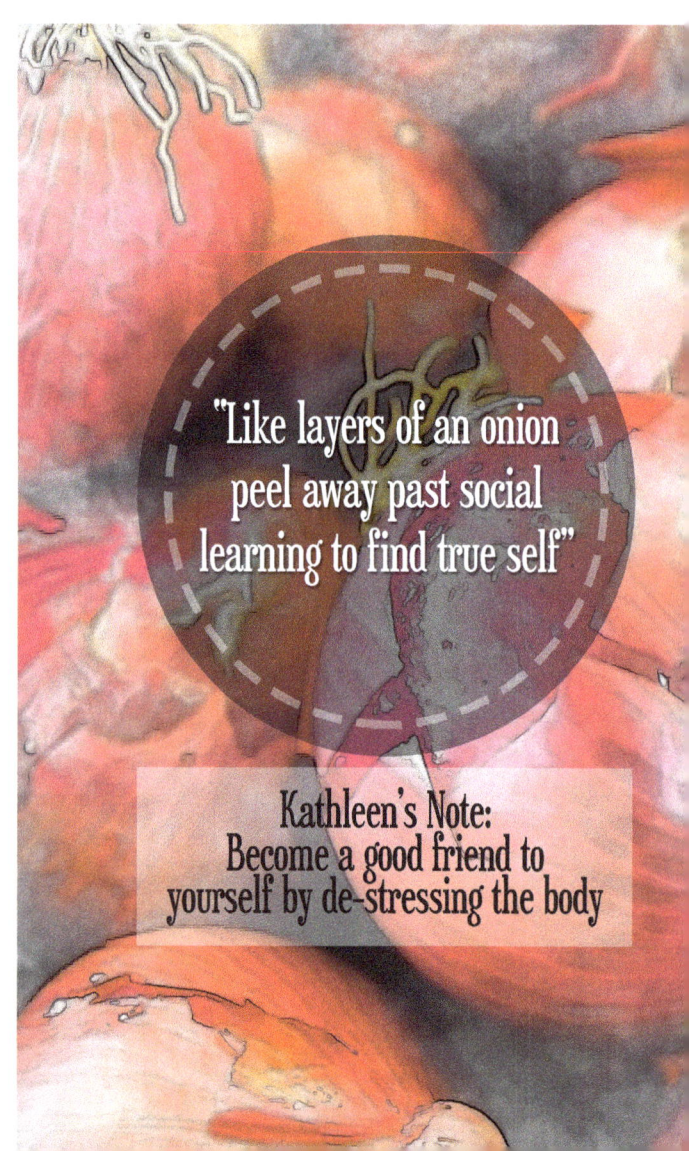

"The secret of having
is all knowing that
you already do"

Kathleen's Note:
Live each moment in time
as a special gift

"Savor every life experience as an opportunity to know true self"

Kathleen's Note:
Become familiar with your strengths and weaknesses through trials and tribulations

"Become aware of your intentions while making life choices"

Kathleen's Note:
Intangible values keep us flowing in the right direction

"Part ways with failure to realize untapped potential for better choices"

Kathleen's Note:
Choose wisely by exploring all options while making life's choices

> "It's your road,
> and yours alone
> Others may walk with
> you, but no one can
> walk it for you"

Kathleen's Note:
Recognize your experience is unique
from which to learn and realize
your strenghts

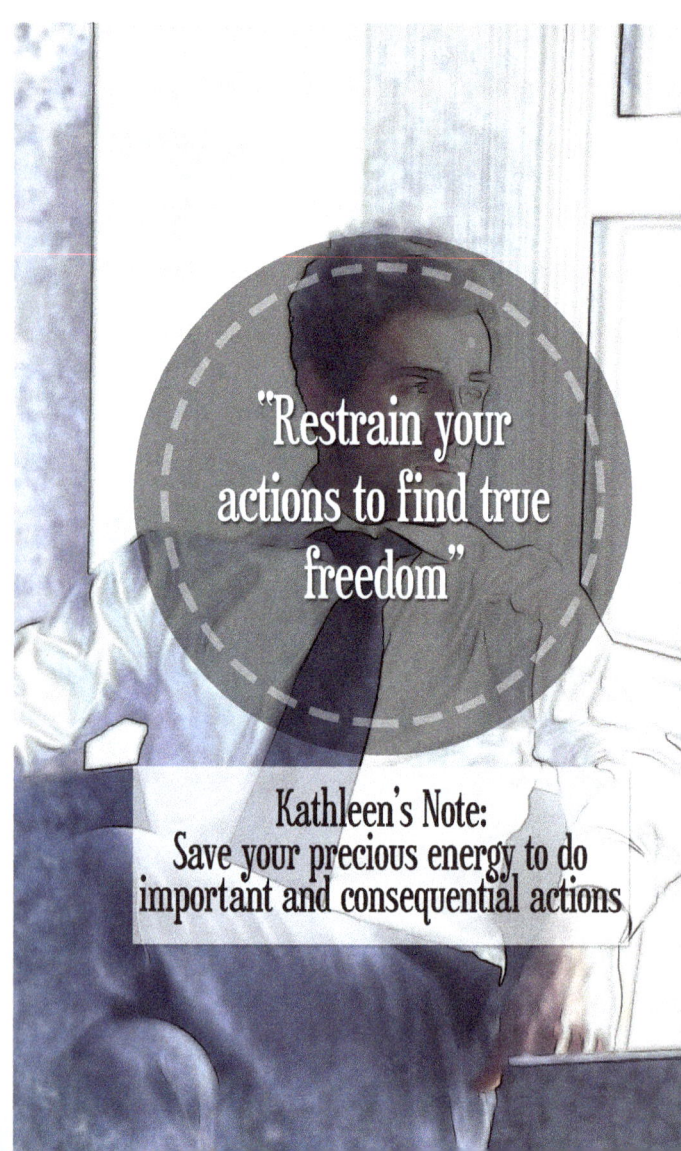

"The search for true self frees one of others' consciousness"

Kathleen's Note:
Your life's journey is your souls' search for new wisdom. Craft it to make conscious decisions with a free mind

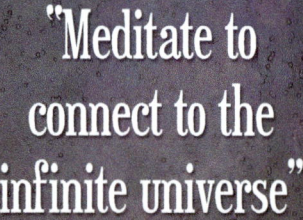

"Meditate to connect to the infinite universe"

Kathleen's Note:
Explore every thought by relating to its reasoning and principles to expand your consciousness

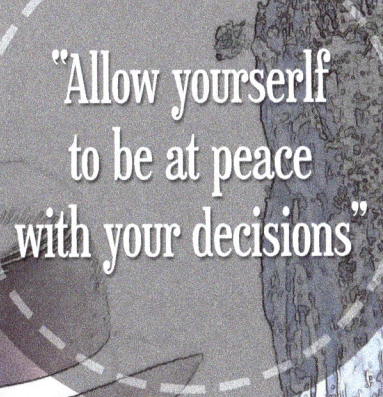

"Strenght lies in complete awareness of self"

Kathleen's Note:
Realize your strenghts and limitations in every situation in assessing the risks you take in your life

THE BEST OF DAILY QUOTES

REDIS-COVER LIVING

"Every Morning is a new beginning"

Kathleen's Note:
Awaken each morning as an opportunity for life

"True creativity is a spiritual exercise"

Kathleen's Note:
Engage the mind to pursue creative work to explore your unique talents

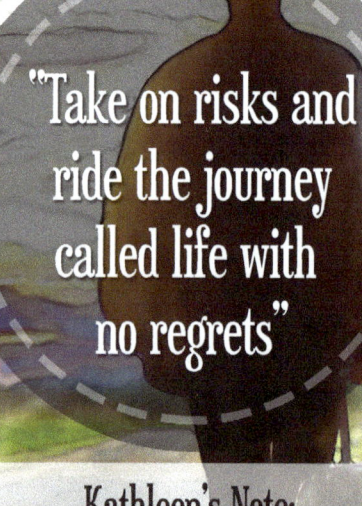

"The journey of life is
not meant to be feared
and planned;
it is meant to be
travelled and enjoyed"

Kathleen's Note:
Dreams are meant to be lived
and experienced in life.
Worry is not a solution

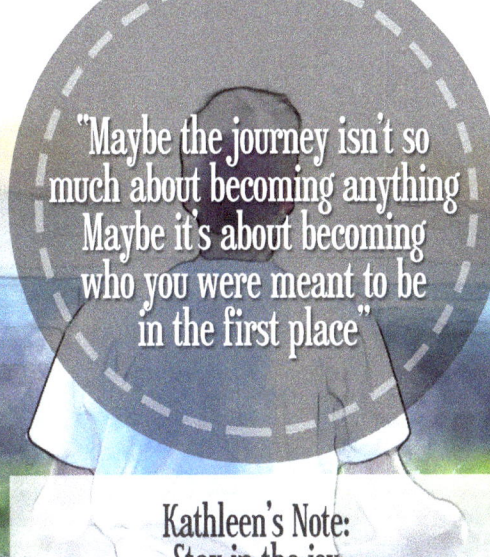

"Maybe the journey isn't so much about becoming anything Maybe it's about becoming who you were meant to be in the first place"

Kathleen's Note:
Stay in the joy of being alive

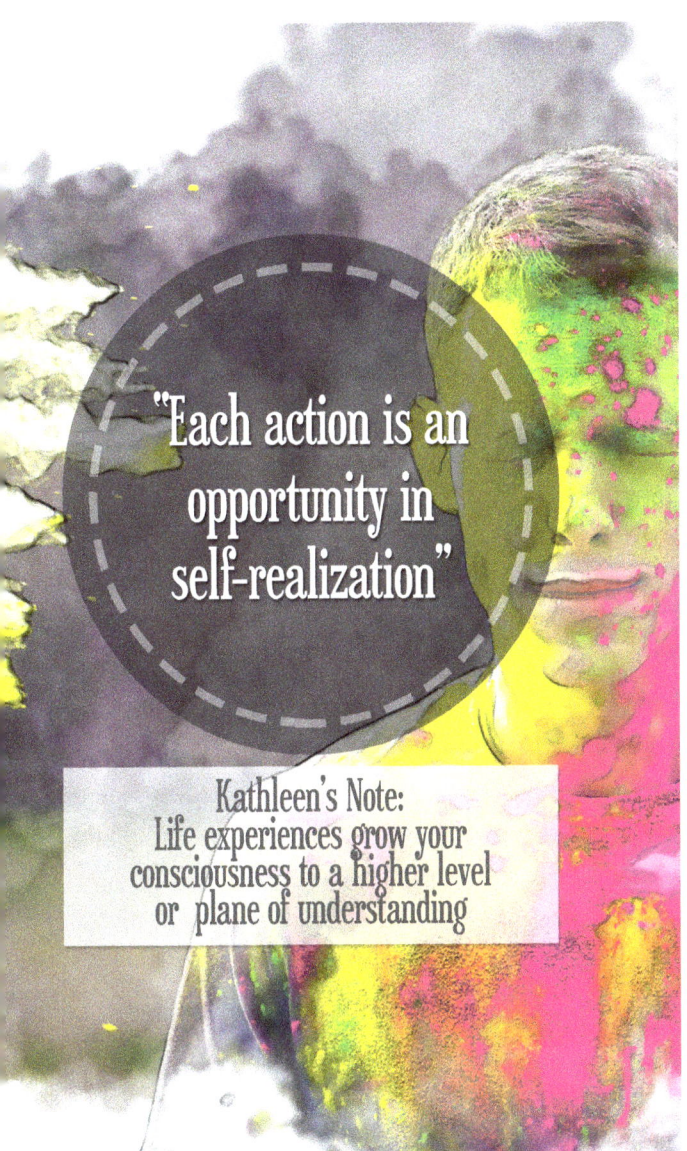

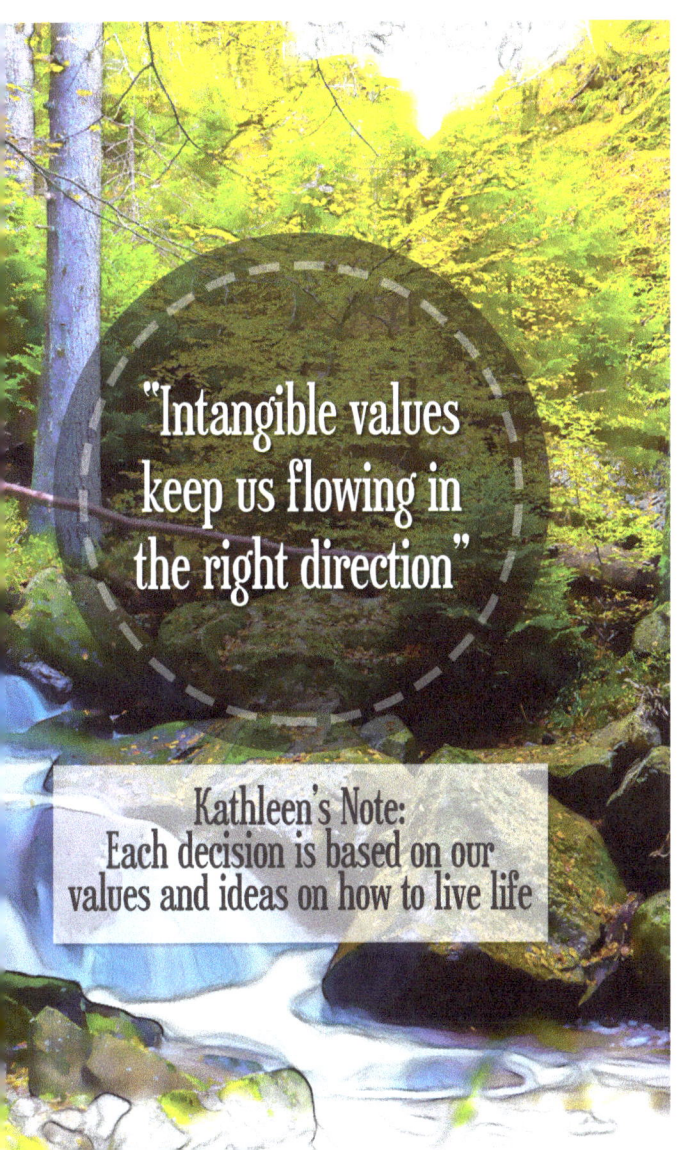

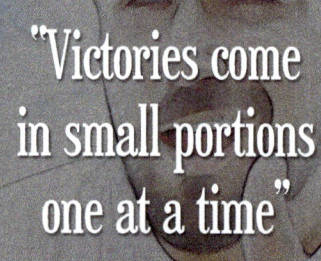

"Victories come in small portions one at a time"

Kathleen's Note:
Savour each success one day at a time

THE BEST OF DAILY QUOTES

INNER
PEACE

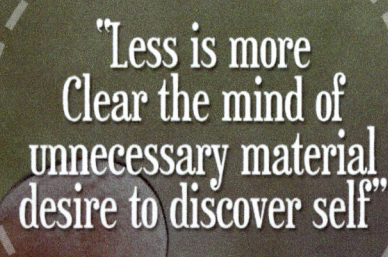

"Less is more
Clear the mind of
unnecessary material
desire to discover self"

Kathleen's Note:
Nurture the mind to
temper ones' desires

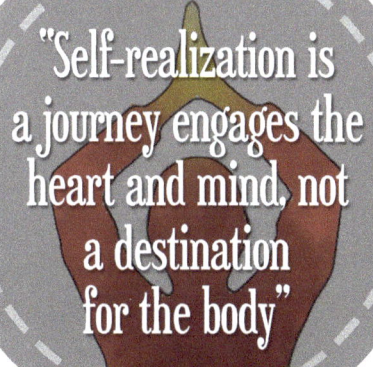

"Self-realization is a journey engages the heart and mind, not a destination for the body"

Kathleen's Note:
Inner peace is an intense, diligent, dedicated and conscious pursuit of refining the mind

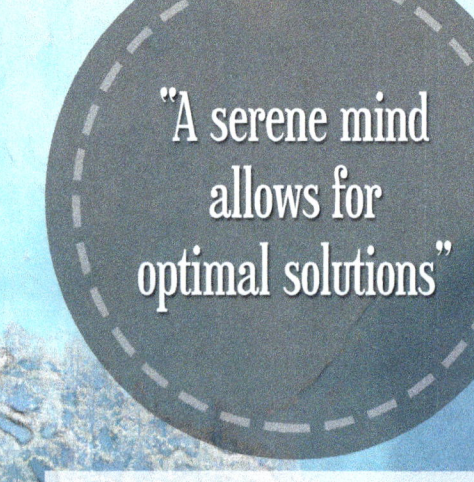

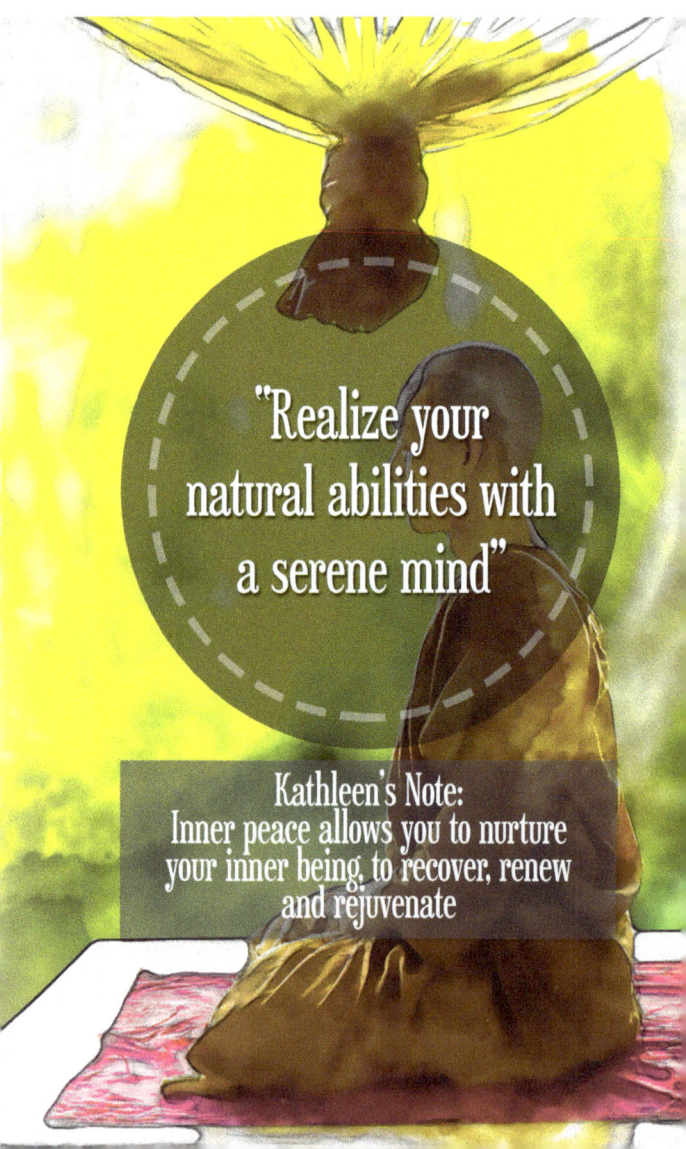

THE BEST OF DAILY QUOTES
SEEK-ING HAPP-INNES

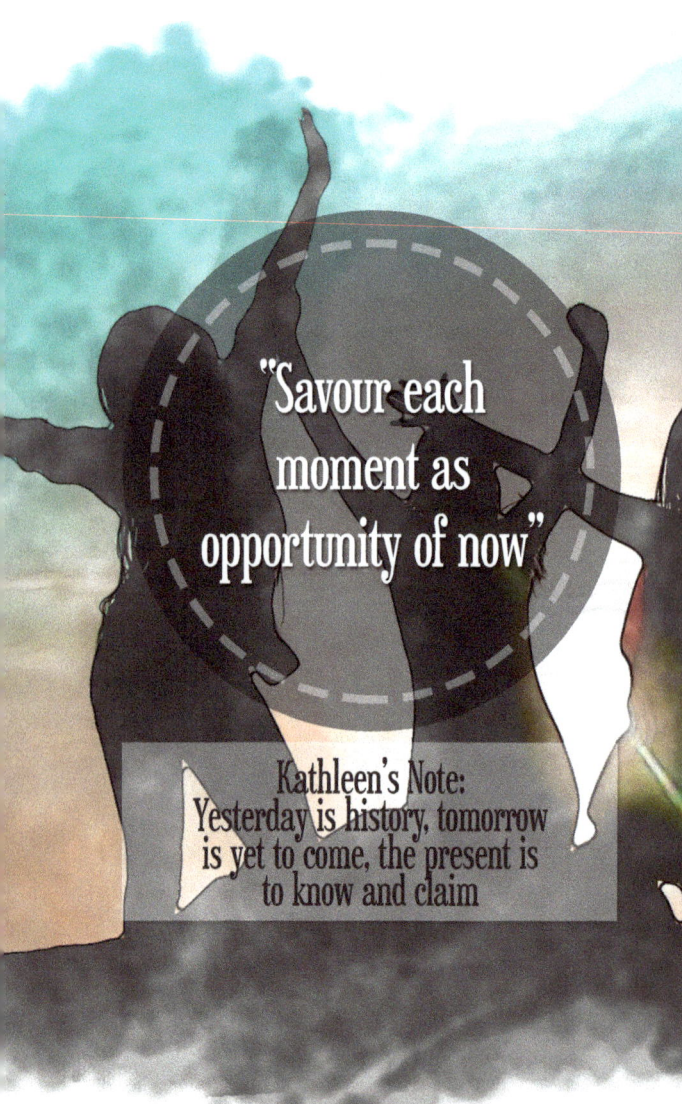

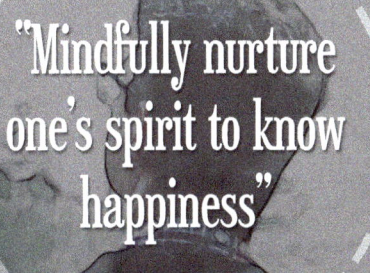

"Mindfully nurture one's spirit to know happiness"

Kathleen's Note:
Feel and know abundance in spirit

"Love brings joy to simple pleasures"

Kathleen's Note:
Live simply to love deeply

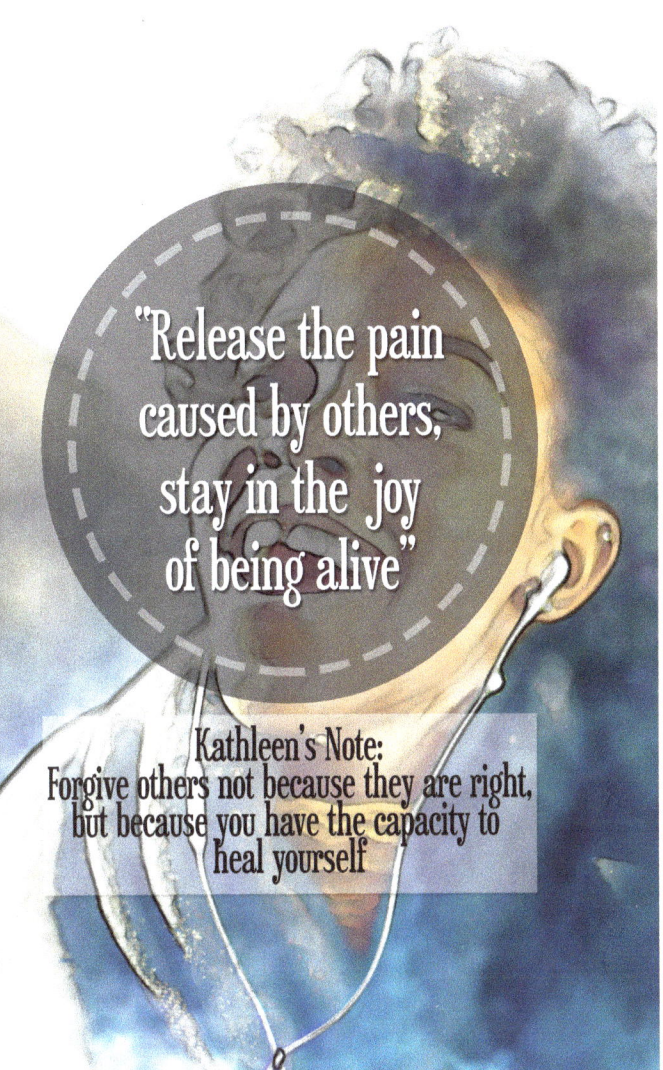

THE BEST OF DAILY QUOTES

ENGAGE THE SOUL

"Relate fully to body, mind, spirit and soul to feel alive"

Kathleen's Note:
Nurture true self to relate and feel your life form

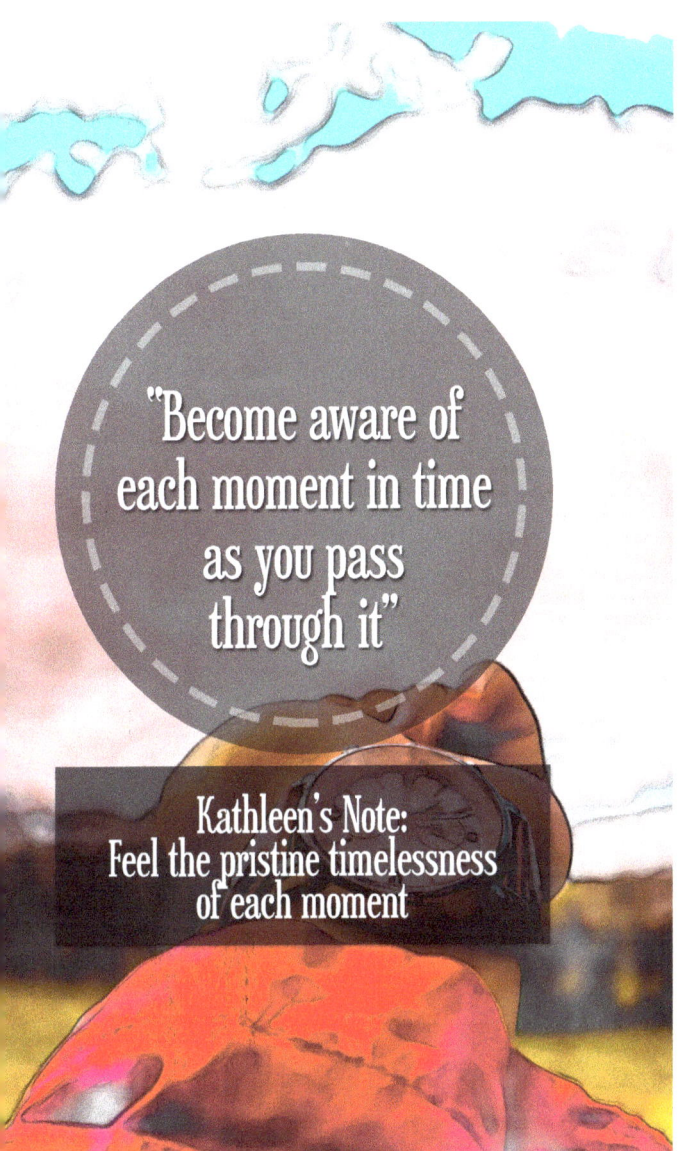

"Breath to feel your life force within and know its unexplored wisdom"

Kathleen's Note:
Calm the mind to connect to the soul. Take deep breaths to nourish and calm the mind

"Enrich the soul
with new ideas
to free yourself
from bondage"

Kathleen's Note:
Every pathway to a successful
life begins with a dream
and imagination

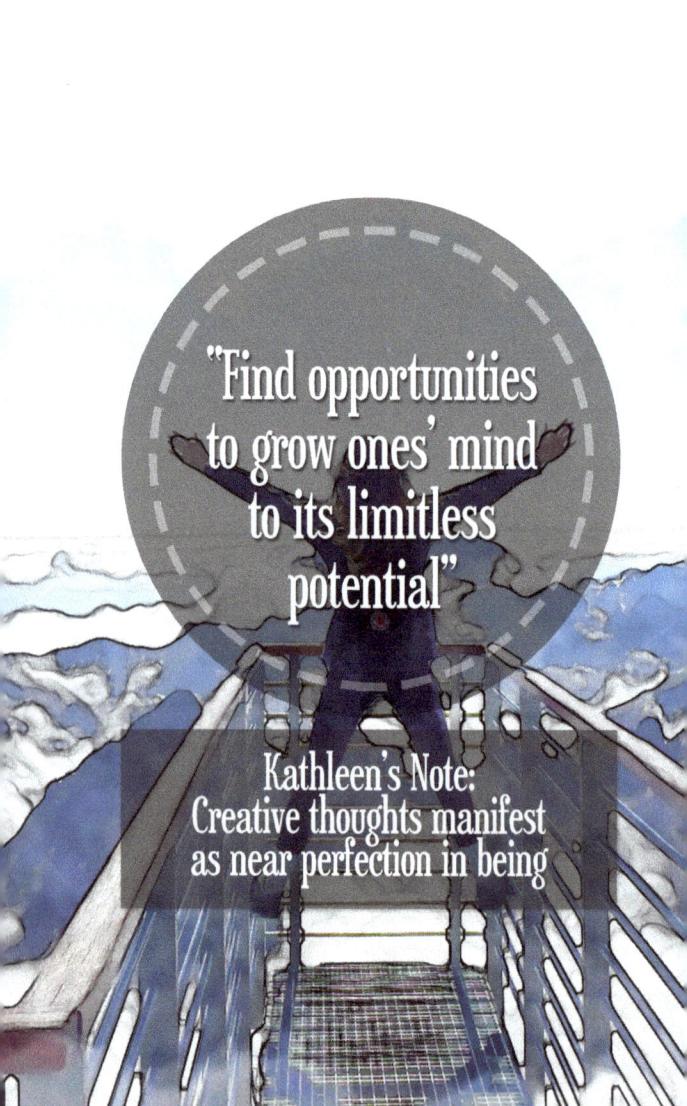

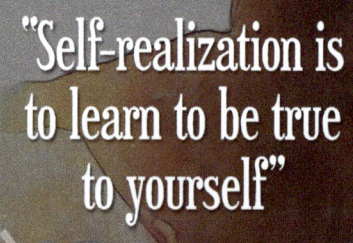

"Self-realization is to learn to be true to yourself"

Kathleen's Note:
Know where you came from in your life's journey to know where you are going.

"Be open to learn from different cultural traditions to seek wisdom from others"

Kathleen's Note:
The power of love extends beyond one lifetime to continuously procreate life

www.ingramcontent.com/pod-product-compliance
Lightning Source LLC
Chambersburg PA
CBHW062113290426
44110CB00023B/2798